# Life in
# High Definition

An Extra-Ordinary Experience
Of Gods Grace In Grief, Loss & Tragedy

## Leonie Allen

First published by Ultimate World Publishing 2025
Copyright © 2025 Leonie Allen

ISBN

Paperback: 978-1-923583-15-3
Ebook: 978-1-923583-16-0

Leonie Allen has asserted her rights under the Copyright, Designs and Patents Act 1988 to be identified as the author of this work. The information in this book is based on the author's experiences and opinions. The publisher specifically disclaims responsibility for any adverse consequences which may result from use of the information contained herein. Permission to use information has been sought by the author. Any breaches will be rectified in further editions of the book.

All rights reserved. No part of this publication may be reproduced, stored in or introduced into a retrieval system, or transmitted in any form, or by any means (electronic, mechanical, photocopying, recording or otherwise) without the prior written permission of the author. Any person who does any unauthorised act in relation to this publication may be liable to criminal prosecution and civil claims for damages. Enquiries should be made through the publisher.

**Cover design:** Daniel W. Allen
**Layout and typesetting:** Ultimate World Publishing
**Editor:** Victoria Pickens

Ultimate World Publishing
Diamond Creek,
Victoria Australia 3089
www.writeabook.com.au

# Testimonials

Our friendship with Leonie and Peter goes back several decades here in Melbourne. It began over coffee in 1995 when their son Shane passed away and, no matter where we fi nd ourselves residing, has continued over the years! The sharing of ourselves in seasons of loss, pain, grief, laughter, tears, coffee catchups, road trips and aeroplane journeys have woven us together in a strong friendship.

Leonie's faith in God has grown and strengthened through these vulnerable seasons she has journeyed. Through the loss of her dear husband, Peter, and two of her sons, Shane and Gerrard.

Leonie's prophetic insight, research, studious mind and delightful way of presenting her life journey will inspire, challenge and probably move to tears and laughter all who read or hear her story.

"A quote we recently read applies to our dear friend, Leonie: "The trials God has brought us through become a platform upon which we can stand and minister to others."

Lady Leonie has a strong, proven platform!

**Graham & Susan McMechan**
**Pastors and friends**
**Melbourne, Australia**

I met Leonie and her late husband Peter more than 25 years ago at a Minister's Conference in Melbourne, Australia. They were an extraordinary couple. Peter was very witty and funny. They complemented each other's ministry.

I don't know of another person that would be as qualified to write on this subject. Leonie has experienced the loss of two adult sons, three grandchildren and her husband of 53 years. She has navigated those seasons of life with grace and courage to continue ministering to hundreds in the body of Christ.

Her message is always one of encouragement, love and comfort that comes from God.

Leonie continues to minister at the invitation of local Pastors and is used by God to bring healing and comfort to broken people.

As a long-time friend and fellow minister, I want to encourage Leonie to continue blessing the Body of Christ.

**Johnny Scroggins**
**Ministers Fellowship International**
**Australasia Director**

Leonie is an amazing woman of God.

We have known each other and ministered together over the past 25 years.

Leonie is the sister of my heart, and we have spent many blessed hours sharing and encouraging each other in the Lord.

Leonie and her husband Peter have been greatly used by God to extend His Kingdom on earth. Now that Peter is in Glory, God is still using Leonie mightily to bless and grow the Body of Christ and bring hope and deliverance to those she ministers to.

**Pastor Olga Kirk**
**Emerald, Central Queensland**

It has been my joy and privilege to know Leonie for the past 7 years. In that time, I have seen firsthand the depth of her heart, the strength of her faith, and the way she carries the love of God into every season of life.

This book is more than words on a page—it is a testimony, a prophetic call, and an invitation. I believe that as you turn each page, the Holy Spirit will meet you in the very place you are, bringing healing, clarity, and fresh courage. These are not just Leonie's stories; they are seeds of hope, destined to take root in the soil of your heart.

I sense that this book will go far beyond its printed pages—carrying restoration into families, freedom into hearts, and vision into futures. May it be a vessel God uses to remind you that your story is not over, and His goodness is still unfolding.

Leonie has poured her life into these pages. My prayer is that as you read, you will encounter the same faithfulness of God that has marked her journey—and that it will mark yours too.

**Pastor Brett Dolley**
**Harvest New Life Church, Pittsworth**

# Contents

Chapter 1: Out Of Breath. Jeremiah 29:11-13 — 9

Chapter 2: NOT AGAIN! Endurance. Isaiah 57:1 — 15

Chapter 3: ANNOUNCING! She's beautiful! — 19

Chapter 4: Romance Blossoms — 27

Chapter 5: Life Changing Encounter. Hebrews 4:12 — 33

Chapter 6: Royal Encounter — 39

Chapter 7: New Frontier. Deuteronomy 8:7 — 45

Chapter 8: OPEN DOOR! Just in Time. Jeremiah 1:5 — 53

Chapter 9: HOMELESS! Survival. Jeremiah 29:11-14 — 61

Chapter 10: Time out. Psalm 71:20-21 — 67

Chapter 11: Mandates and Mayhem! Jeremiah 15:20 — 71

Chapter 12: The Adventure Continues. Philippians 4:8 — 79

About the Author — 83

# Dedication

I am Proud to dedicate this book to the man I shared the journey with for 53 years before his promotion to Glory, my dear husband Peter and to the six fine sons we were blessed with. They're all very talented in their own field, but I'm particularly proud of my youngest son Dan using his graphic art skills to produce the striking cover for this book.

Chapter 1

# Out Of Breath.
## Jeremiah 29:11-13

# Life in High Definition

'We cannot get a camera down your throat; you need to go to the Hospital immediately!' With these shocking words to my husband Peter and myself from the Ear, Nose and Throat Specialist, our lives were dramatically changed.

A tracheotomy needed to be performed to open Peter's airway, otherwise he would suffocate, to be followed by tests to determine the cause of the obstruction.

We arrived at the emergency Department of the local hospital where we waited for several hours. Following triage, we were told that the Doctor on duty had been called to an emergency but would return soon. Thirty minutes later, the doctor arrived, and she proceeded to try and insert a camera into Peter's throat.

She exclaimed, 'Oh, my God!' quickly grabbed her mobile phone, and said into it, 'Get me a bed for this patient, STAT!'

Peter was settled into a bed opposite the nurses' station, then an Anaesthetist came to explain that if Peter stopped breathing during the night, then he would come and puncture a hole in the front of his throat using a pen-like object!

As Peter was under constant observation, I drove home with my mind reeling. Thoughts came immediately of my dear dad who died suddenly at just age fifty.

Surely this could not happen to my darling husband. I didn't sleep, instead I spent the night searching online for the meaning of tracheotomy/tracheostomy. In the morning, Peter was the first into the theatre, and I waited for several hours before I was able to see him. He had a filter taped around his throat and could not talk. We tried to communicate with him by having him write on paper, but

## Out Of Breath. Jeremiah 29:11-13

that was difficult, so we purchased a child's erasable doodle board, which was a bit easier for him.

The next day when the surgeon came around, Peter asked (wrote), 'What took you so long? I was awake the whole time?'

> Tracheotomy means the procedure for opening the trachea in front of the throat. Tracheostomy means the opening itself.

She said, 'What do you mean?'

He wrote, 'In the movies, they just punch a hole.'

She then explained that they had to do the operation very slowly as they did not know exactly where the tumour was. Because of the obstruction, they could not anaesthetise him as he would die, so that's why he was awake during the whole operation until they reached the trachea and could insert a tube. She explained that it would be 3 or 4 weeks before doing the total laryngectomy (removal of the voice box) as they needed to get some scans done to determine exactly where and how big the tumour was.

Some advice I can offer to anyone living with someone struggling with a persistent cough and/or shortness of breath is to ask for a second opinion if you are not sure of the treatment being offered. Our doctor had explained that medically, any persistent throat condition is usually related to people who smoke cigarettes or drink alcohol. Due to Peter not fitting the profile for those conditions, he wasn't reviewed for 18 months.

I became a nurse and carer overnight! Keeping the filter clean and generally ensuring that Peter was okay. After scans showing the tumour was hidden in the muscle wall of the larynx, the only option was to remove the entire larynx. The surgery was scheduled for the end of November 2007.

My husband was the Pastor of our local church and a preacher, so losing his voice was devastating.

Through my online research, I discovered numerous medical papers written about laryngectomies. One cause of tumours developing in the throat, is unresolved grief (not releasing the pain and heartache through tears and/or talking) which causes the vocal cords to tighten. Left untreated, this can alter the molecular structure of the larynx, leading to tumours developing.

We had experienced several tragedies of loss and death in the family during the years leading up to this situation. With the death of our first grandchild, Jessica, who was the daughter of our son Chris and his partner Ilka, on the day she was born in 1990. Followed by the death of our third son, Shane, in a freak accident in 1995. Then the death of another grandchild, Jackson, the second son of Daniel and Catherine, who died of cot death (SIDS) at 3 months old. And then Peter's dear mother, who lived to the wonderful age of ninety-six, passed away. He was her only son, and he loved her dearly. In Western culture, men typically do not grieve openly. And I realised that this was one of the reasons why Peter had developed this tumour because of holding in the pain and tears of all the loss and tragedy.

My first sight of Peter after the operation was such a shock, it took my breath away as the suture line was the same as on our son Shane after the autopsy! I quickly checked that he was actually breathing. He was, Praise God.

We began a new regimen that consisted of Peter having to breathe in steam from hot water over a bowl daily to keep the trachea moist.

## Out Of Breath. Jeremiah 29:11-13

Initially, he sat with a towel over his head, breathing in the steam until a nurse came in and said, 'You don't need to cover your whole head, it only needs to go into your throat!'

He was released from the hospital in the second week of December. And we began adjusting to our new life. As he hadn't had a valve fitted yet, we had to arrange appointments with a speech pathologist to rectify this.

The day we attended an appointment to have the valve inserted, there were measurements taken, and the speech pathologist was showing me how this procedure would be done and explaining that I could do this. I said, "But I'm not medically trained."

She replied, 'Well, you've had six children, so you should know a thing or two.'

Immediately she had the valve inserted into Peter's throat, then her pager went off and she left, needing to respond to that. When she walked out of the room, Peter covered the tracheostomy and said, 'I love you.'

I burst into tears.

The speech pathologist came back and asked, 'What's wrong?'

'He just told me he loved me,' I replied.

'You what! Count to five,' she replied.

From there, Peter proceeded to count to ten, and the speech pathologist said, 'I've never seen that happen with somebody who has newly had a valve inserted.' However, we were able to explain that he had been a brass bandsman and had learnt breath control from the diaphragm, which made it easier for him to speak.

The action of covering the trachea enabled him to force air through the valve. He could speak! It was wonderful to hear his voice again, even though it was slightly husky, after weeks of not hearing him speak.

Chapter 2

# NOT AGAIN!
# Endurance.
# Isaiah 57:1

## Life in High Definition

At the time of Peter's surgery, we were living in the same house with our youngest son, Daniel and his wife and their two boys. They went away on holiday for two weeks prior to Christmas, which gave us a week to adjust to this new way of living on our own.

On Christmas Eve, we decided to attend the midnight service with our friend, the Reverend Suzanne Chambers, and she was such a blessing because during the communion service, she laid hands on us both and prayed. And we believe it was a prophetic action for what was to come.

Our son and family arrived home a week later stating: 'It was too hot, not enough water and too many flies.' Our son Damian, who lived in NSW with his wife and family, including their newest addition, Hannah Rose, born on July 31$^{st}$, were going to come down for a visit in the New Year, but decided to come early due to the traffic conditions. So, on the day before New Year's Eve, we were all together when our son Gerrard came over. He was borrowing Daniel's motorbike to go for a day's ride with friends the next day. We enjoyed a couple of hours chatting, talking, and playing with the children, then we all waved him goodbye.

The next morning, the unthinkable happened. The phone rang, it was Kaylene, our daughter-in-law and Gerrard's wife. Gerrard had been killed in a freak road accident. *Not again! Not again!* I felt like my heart stopped beating for a couple of seconds. This was all Deja vu from 1995, when our third son, Shane, was killed in a freak accident.

I went into our bedroom and cried out to God. How could this happen? How could this happen? And I was immediately prompted to look in the Bible at **Isaiah 57:1**.

## Isaiah 57:1

Gerrard was a fine Christian man, very involved in his local church, a loving husband, and a devoted father to his son, Connor. Gerrard was a man who was always willing to help others who were struggling. It didn't seem fair that he was gone. Yet I knew with God's promise he had already gone to heaven. He had been the tender-hearted one of our boys, always caring and concerned about other people, so I believe that there are some things coming into the world that God was protecting him from.

> **Isaiah 57:1** *Good people pass away, the godly often die before their time, but no one seems to care or wonder why. No one seems to understand that God is protecting them from the evil to come.*

What was to have been a time of enjoying our grandchildren and time with our sons and their wives became a time of planning a funeral and a celebration of a life cut short.

Gerrard's local church community were very supportive and helpful, and only too happy to allow us to use the building to have the celebration of his life. We were so blessed that hundreds of people turned up to honour this young man who had just faithfully gone about helping everyone he could and using his skills and abilities in the workplace.

Many of the men that he had helped and walked alongside stood up to testify at his life celebration, sharing his support and help when they were in a hard place. I found these things encouraging when your heart is broken.

## Life in High Definition

Within a week, due to the stress and grief we had experienced, Peter's neck swelled up and he developed Cellulitis. He was immediately admitted back into the hospital and put on tube feeding, not allowed to eat anything. His droll sense of humour had him sharing that it was difficult for him; the only things on TV during the day were cooking shows.

Peter was in the hospital for a whole month when we received an invitation to go to New Zealand to celebrate the 50$^{th}$ wedding anniversary of his oldest sister, June, and her husband. We made arrangements to get there, much to the horror of the surgeon who said it was far too soon for him to be travelling, but we went anyway. It was good to spend time with family.

Which leads us back to our family origins.

Chapter 3

# ANNOUNCING! She's beautiful!

# Life in High Definition

I am a Baby Boomer. Born just after the Second World War, the oldest of eleven children.

After me, there were six boys; Clive, Laurence, Kevin, Thomas, Robin, Martin (Martin died the day he was born), then two more girls, Judith and Therese, one boy named Paul, then my baby sister Carmel who is twelve years and ten months younger than me!

After I was born, Dad was apparently reluctant to go to the nursery to see me; he was hoping for a boy! Mum insisted that he see me, and he came back grinning, saying, 'She's beautiful and the only one not crying!'

As I grew up, my role, being a girl, was always to help Mum. Cleaning, making beds, washing dishes, and other household chores. When I tried to make my brothers help, their response was, "You're not the boss of me!" so I became a tomboy to tried and fit in with their games and activities.

My sense of self was not good. With thick and incredibly straight hair, I felt very plain. With an unusual (for that time) name, I tried to 'fit in' but experienced a lot of rejection.

This led to a very painful experience. One day after leaving school, a one-room country school on the West Coast of New Zealand's South Island, I was running to try and keep up with kids on their bikes. They stopped, grabbed small rocks from the gravel road and began pelting me with them. I attempted to flee, but one rock caught me in the middle of my back and sent me sprawling, unconscious on the road.

This all happened outside one of the farmhouses and the mother of the house came out to see what was going on, she carried me to the house then rang my mum on the party line phone (rural telephone

## ANNOUNCING! She's beautiful!

systems operated on one line with each subscriber having a separate call ring i.e. *short, long, short or long, short, long, like morse code*). As we were fifteen miles from the nearest Doctor, I was just taken home and put to bed to recover.

A week later, I experienced a very humiliating event when my mum took me to the school, made me stand between her and the teacher in front of the whole school and demanded to know who had done this to me. I had scabs on my face, hands and knees from sprawling on the road. I knew who the ringleaders were, so I stared hard at them, but no one spoke. They knew that I could point them out, but when I didn't, it gave me power over them. I was determined there and then that I would never let them bully me again, and I was seven years old.

Years later, there was a wonderful experience relating to this event, but I will come back to that.

The years of living on the farm came to an end in 1957 when we moved to Nelson at the top of the South Island. Mum decided I needed to become more 'lady-like' so she enrolled me at the Convent School in Nelson, although we lived in Richmond, which was almost nine miles away. To save on bus fares, this meant I had to ride my bike, which often made me late for school.

My baby sister was born in 1958, and I had to stay home from school to look after the family while Mum was in the hospital as Dad was working. Some of the ladies in the Church helped with meals, but it was a lot of responsibility for a twelve-year-old.

The next two years were busy, happy and scary. I was like a second mum to my baby sister after my mum weaned her. One event that stands out from those days relates to the tree house that my brothers and I built in the big pine tree at the back of our property. We could climb up the tree but used a rope to haul things up. We tied a sack on the rope, loaded my sister into it, 4 or 5 months old at the time, and had her in the treehouse. She began to cry, and Mum couldn't work out where the crying was coming from. We all got a hiding after that event!

The scary part of those years was Mum having three miscarriages. One happened in the kitchen, and I had to send my brothers to call the doctor, then clean up all the blood before the rest of them saw it. My mum lost so much blood that when Dad finally got her to the hospital, she was transfused with six pints of blood. She then had to have surgery. All this resulted in me having more time off school to look after the family at just 14.

## Developing Practical Skills

During my teenage years, I taught myself to sew on an old treadle sewing machine Mum was given. I didn't get new clothes as there were five boys after me, so I wore hand-me-downs that we received from other families with girls my age. I earned the money working in a market garden on the weekends and holidays to buy materials. Mum didn't like sewing but was a prolific knitter. For my 16$^{th}$ birthday, my dad decided that I could have a new electric sewing machine...JOY!

My dad was of the generation that didn't think it was worthwhile for girls to have a tertiary education. His comment, 'Girls just get married and have babies!' So, I left school at fifteen to work in an exclusive women's shoe shop (stilettoes were all the rage), developing a love of shoes.

## ANNOUNCING! She's beautiful!

Because of low pay, I looked for other work, doing a few months at a local nursing home, then found a position as receptionist/telephonist at a manufacturing company, Zip Industries. I loved doing the switchboard work and was hastily learning how to manage the equipment. A delegation from the New Zealand Post Office, which handled all telephone communications at that time, came to check my work—I was 'headhunted'. They offered me a job as a telephonist, and I began my new job in the city, requiring me to do shift work.

As I had obtained my driver's licence at fifteen, Dad allowed me to take the family car to work when I was on a late shift, as the last bus from the city left before I finished my shift.

Due to the social environment in the city in those years, you were either in the party hard, drinking crowd, or the go to the movies and be home by 10:30 crowd; I didn't fit into either of them. At the age of 17, I applied for a transfer to Dunedin, which Dad approved of as my grandparents were there. I moved into a flat with four other girls and enjoyed a year of independence and fun. Fitting in occasional visits to my grandparents and my godparents, who lived in Dunedin, too. It was very hard being away from my family for Christmas, especially as I had to work the morning shift, and my cousins didn't remember to pick me up after work to spend some time with my grandparents! Through my work I met a guy, and we began dating.

A year later, my parents moved from Nelson to Timaru, buying a 'milk bar' and catering business and asked me to come and work for them. I packed up and relocated to Timaru known as The Riviera of the South, being a seaside city.

As my parents and nine siblings lived in the accommodation above the shop, there was no room for me, so I boarded with a lady from the local parish. Dad would pick me up every morning when he made

# Life in High Definition

his bakery run. Life was busy. The guy I had been dating would take the train from Dunedin every couple of weeks to spend time with me.

In the meantime, guys from the local trucking company would come to the shop for morning tea or lunch, and one of them said to me, 'You should take pity on this guy (Peter), he doesn't have a girlfriend, take him to the movies!' So, I did.

We began to date on a regular basis. Peter invited me to an end-of-year function for the brass band he played in. The guy from Dunedin turned up that weekend, unexpectedly. I didn't know what to do as Peter was away working that afternoon. I asked my dad for the car so I could go and see Peter after he finished work. Dad wanted to know what my answer was going to be. When I told him that I would go with Peter, he said, 'Leave the other bloke to me, I'll sort him out.' We went off to the function where the other guy turned up as well with an engagement ring. It was quite embarrassing. But I realised that I needed to spend time with Peter as I had come to really like him.

It became obvious that Dad preferred Peter, so we began going steady in December. Peter went to spend Christmas with his family, but he had been invited to a New Year celebration at a friend's place in another town near us, and I was invited to join him. Mum and Dad allowed me to go as there were other married couples who would be suitable chaperones!

Everyone was in party mode on New Year's Eve, when Peter's friend Jim said, 'You don't want to let this one get away. Go outside and make a decision!'

We were ushered out to the front steps and left alone. Peter looked at me sitting on the steps and asked, 'What about it?'

## ANNOUNCING! She's beautiful!

That was my proposal!

We sealed it with a kiss, then went back into the party and announced we were engaged to cheers and hugs all around!

Returning home two days later, we arrived at the shop and settled in the kitchen. Dad asked how the weekend was. Peter pulled me onto his knee and said, 'It was good; we got engaged!'

Dad had a big smile on his face, saying, 'That's great, when are you getting married?' while Mum began banging dishes in the sink! We said we wanted to wait six months, which Mum seemed to settle a bit with that information (she had thought I was pregnant!).

Dad said to Peter, 'We need to seal this with a drink, come to the pub with me.' When they came back, Peter looked rather green in the face as Dad had given him whiskey, something he didn't normally drink, but you don't say no to your future father-in-law!

As Peter's parents lived in Wellington, we decided to visit them for a week over the Easter break. We travelled on the overnight ferry from Christchurch to Wellington, and they met us at the Ferry Terminal. Peter's Mum gave me a hug and immediately said, 'You may call us Mum and Dad.' It was so lovely to be accepted. She was a real encouragement to me throughout our marriage.

Chapter 4

# Romance Blossoms

## Life in High Definition

Back home again, the New Zealand Winter was heavily settling in. We needed to find somewhere to live as Peter was sharing a flat with other guys and I was boarding in a private home. We found a one-bedroom flat which was half of an older cottage-style house and Peter moved in before the wedding. The other half of the cottage was rented to an English woman named Florence Amelia Bartlett, known to the family as Mrs B, who became a dear friend and eventually the godmother of our firstborn son, Michael.

We continued with our wedding plans, meeting with the local priest, who happened to be the parish priest in Nelson when I was attending the convent school! We planned to be married at the Basilica in the city on the 11th of June 1966.

I modified the dress I made to wear as a debutante while I was living in Dunedin, adding sleeves and a train. The wedding took place with family, relatives, godparents, and friends. Some of them thought I was crying during the ceremony as my veil was shaking, but I was laughing at Peter who was making faces at me while the priest had his back turned! The sun emerged from behind the clouds as we stepped out of the Basilica, now man and wife. After a lovely reception with our family and friends, we had a dance party at night for all the friends we had not been able to invite to the reception. My baby sister, our flower girl, insisted on dancing with Peter, so he picked her up and whirled her around the room!

We went on our honeymoon to visit friends who had not been able to attend the wedding due to her advanced stage of pregnancy, and they insisted we stay at their house. The next morning, she came and roused us saying, 'Peter, can you please go and find my husband? The baby is coming.' We ended up looking after their eleven-month-old child until the grandmother could arrive. It was great practise for starting our own family.

# Romance Blossoms

We settled into married life with me working at my family's milk bar, and Peter at the trucking company. Life was full and busy for the first six months. We celebrated my 20th birthday with friends over, eating some of the very sticky pavlova I had made (sticky due to me still learning how to cook on a woodfired stove!) and the following day I had stomach pains that became more and more intense.

Peter called the doctor, who checked me out, then called an ambulance, sending me to the hospital to have my appendix out. I can remember the staff laughing and giggling outside the curtains around my bed when they discussed the fact that my breakfast had been leftover Pavlova! This was a very difficult time as I had just become used to sleeping with somebody in the bed next to me and had quickly ended up in the hospital for ten days. Back home recovering from this surgery, I realised at some point that I had become pregnant but due to my disrupted cycle, I was not aware until I experienced an early miscarriage. Then I conceived again, and soon we were able to tell our parents.

This was the first grandchild for my parents, and Peter's parents were hoping, of course, that it would be a boy to carry on the family name. In due course, Michael Anthony Allen was born on the 5th of November, Guy Faulks Day, 1967! It was obvious due to his size and being covered in vernix (the substance on a baby's skin in utero) that he was an early baby weighing just five and a half pounds (2.5 kg). However, he gained weight rapidly, thriving on breastmilk! With the news of his birth, there was great rejoicing from both sets of grandparents.

Then followed the birth of Christopher on the 2nd of March 1969. Thirteen months later, on the 11th of May 1970, Shane was born. Followed by Gerrard on the 8th of August 1971, then Damian on the 4th of January 1973, another miscarriage, then Daniel on the 19th of July 1974.

## Life in High Definition

Damian's birth created a stir. As he was born at home and Peter delivered him. Peter had been working on the car that day, so it was out of action for several hours. When I told him I thought I was in labour he asked if I wanted him to call the ambulance. I said, 'No, it will be okay for a while.' But things moved very quickly.

My sister Judy and her boyfriend were visiting that day. She walked me up to the bedroom, and he rode his motorbike out to the road as we were living in the country, to direct the ambulance which Peter had called in the meantime. Damian made his appearance.

We were taken to the maternity hospital by ambulance. And when they tried to pick him up and carry him away, I said, 'You can't take him. He is still attached to me!' (When Damian was born, Peter tied a slipknot in the cord as we had nothing sterile to cut the cord with!) So, the staff tied and cut the cord before weighing him.

During my stay at the maternity hospital. The nursing sister was calling on me to help other mothers establish their breastfeeding relationships, and that began a whole new area of learning for me. Training to become a lactation consultant. My credentials arrived the day Daniel was born and that was a red-letter day! I had wanted to have a home birth as I had with Damian, but due to my dad passing away just three weeks before, my doctor arrived at the door that morning telling me he was concerned about me going overdue and wanted to help get this baby out safely. After a busy day packing and getting the other boys settled with friends, I arrived at the maternity hospital that night to find I was not expected as my doctor had forgotten to notify the staff I was coming! I said I would go back home but one of my friends was midwife on duty that night, so she rang my doctor who assured her that he would be in to see me soon. When he came, he did a small procedure and assured me I would have my baby by breakfast time next morning! Without any prior labour and just Peter beside me, I delivered my huge ten-pound (4.5kg) baby just thirty minutes later!

Life was very busy raising my six lovely boys. Noisy, lots of cooking, cleaning and washing. Leading meetings for pregnant and nursing mothers, involved in groups in our Parish. Then a medical situation developed, stage 1 cervical cancer. I needed to have surgery, a hysterectomy. There would be no more babies.

Chapter 5

# Life Changing Encounter.
# Hebrews 4:12

# Life in High Definition

Life was challenging after a major surgery. I needed help at home as I still had three preschoolers. The young woman who was sent to help me was glowing, and I asked her if she was a charismatic Christian. She explained she went to a local church and had the good sense to talk to an older lady in her church as she realised I was a reader. She came armed with several books of testimonies from Christians who had experienced a revelation and a relationship with Jesus, the Son of God. As I read these books, I noticed they all had a particular prayer at the at the back of them. So, I read this prayer, lay down and went to sleep. When I woke up in the morning, my whole world had changed. Everything seemed new, fresh, green, and light. This was the beginning of my journey in a relationship with Jesus as my Lord and Saviour.

The first 'rhema' (live to me) scripture I received was:

> **Hebrews 4:12** *The Word of God is living and active and sharper than any two-edged sword, cutting between soul and spirit, between joint and marrow, for the discerning of the thoughts and intentions of the heart.*

This became my foundational scripture for my new faith journey.

An interesting aside to this experience was that I had been raised in a household that used what would have been termed colourful language. Not realising that this was not what other people used in their common or regular speech. The most dramatic thing that happened in this encounter with Jesus was that I never used that type of language again. And this was an eye opener to my dear husband, Peter, who in turn committed himself to being a follower of Jesus.

## Life Changing Encounter. Hebrews 4:12

One event in that first year of my new life was having a car accident. One rainy day, I was taking a young friend back to her home, and a young woman rear-ended our Volkswagen Kombi, sending us into the gutter on the side of the road. Daniel was in the back of the vehicle, and on impact, the door was knocked off, causing him to fall out into the road. I was distraught that he might have been hurt, but he just had a little scratch on him from some of the broken glass. unfortunately, our vehicle was a write-off because the Kombi has the engine in the rear compartment. Because of the terrible language the other young driver was using, my young friend was sitting on the gutter with her hands over Daniel's ears, protecting him from hearing the colourful language. I had to go through a process of learning to forgive and release somebody from my judgment because of that experience. It was an incredibly valuable lesson in my early Christian Walk.

Our life took on a whole new dimension of discovery, learning, training, attending different church services, and being involved with a group called Emmanuel Singers where we regularly sang at church services and even public events. It was a joyful time; making new friends, discovering whole new areas of life that we had never realised we were surrounded by. In the middle of all this, of course, we were raising our sons and getting them ready for school. Eventually, all six of them attended the same primary school, which was a notable achievement for that particular school.

The year following my surgery. We took on a student through our Parish who had come to New Zealand on a scholarship. Alexander Ma'afu Tu'itavake was from Tonga, and he lived with us for nearly five years. We also hosted some students from Western Samoa who were in our city on scholarships. They were the cousins of a girl who had stayed with us for some time during her pregnancy in 1973. These three students, twins —a boy and a girl—and their older sister would come and stay at our place during the school holidays.

# Life in High Definition

We would attend the Pentecostal Church in our town at the evening service, and our boys would be tucked into their sleeping bags under the row of chairs in front of us. We learnt very quickly about reading the Bible. Discovering all the promises God had made to those who believed in Him. This was an exciting time that led us to take on a study to help understand what the Bible was speaking about. I eventually obtained a Diploma in Theology in 1985. We were hosting a charismatic prayer meeting in our home, which grew from around twelve attendees to nearly forty. It got crowded, but we saw many answers to prayer—people healed, were restored, and grew in faith.

We were invited by the coordinators to continue to host a prayer meeting in our home while they hosted one in their home as well. They had taken a year's break due to the arrival of a new child in their family.

Peter and I had a sense that we were coming to a time of change in our lives, so we said, 'God show us by Christmas what we are to do?'

We were invited on Christmas Day to go for morning tea with some friends who had moved into our town. They had been going to another local church but believed they were to start a Church themselves and invited us to join them. This was a significant step for us. But we agreed.

We became the Timaru Community Church, and it was a steep learning curve for us in our discovery of what being Pentecostal really meant. And through learning about the gifts and the work of the Holy Spirit, I became a worship singer, and we were engaged in the leadership and planning, running meetings and teaching people. Those were great times with lots of celebration, where we saw new people coming to faith, and saw people engage in singing and worship. We had the experience of somebody listening to the

## Life Changing Encounter. Hebrews 4:12

singing out in the street, coming in and responding to an invitation to surrender their life to Jesus.

My childhood experience of being stoned and left unconscious and the subsequent decision of never being taken advantage of again led me to seek some prayerful help for my difficulties in relationships. As a friend prayed with me, I realised some forgiveness was needed, and this caused a real change in my attitude and the way I related to people. A wonderful outcome. Freedom from the pain of the experience from so many years earlier.

Chapter 6

# Royal Encounter

## Life in High Definition

As Peter and I continued our journey of discovery in our new Christian Walk, we both became involved with Christian groups—me with Women's Aglow, and Peter with Full Gospel Businessmen's International. These groups had a national conference every year in New Zealand, and we enjoyed attending them. In 1982, the conference was held in Auckland, so we decided to drive there. We also decided that, as we were already so far along on the journey, we would fly over to Tonga to meet Alex's family. And then go on to Western Samoa to meet the family of the students we had hosted in our home in 1974 and 1975. This was a very interesting experience.

We met some Christian folk in Tonga, and they invited us to a weeknight prayer meeting at the royal residence. We walked in there, not knowing that we were expected, and were led to some chairs that had been placed there for us. At the end of the prayer meeting, one of the servants in the home came and invited us to come up to the Dais where the Prince Regent, the host of the prayer meeting, was going to have a cup of tea, and had invited us to join him. It was such an honour and a privilege.

The interesting thing was, according to royal protocol, no one could be above the eye line of the royal personage, so the servants who were bringing the cups of tea out to us had to come on their knees to deliver it. This was a new experience for us. The prince was interested in football, rugby football, and wanted to have a discussion with Peter about the status of the New Zealand team and ask about our children and the reason that we were in Tonga. He thanked us very much for looking after one of their people, Alex, when he was in our country. Overall, it was a most memorable experience.

One of the Prince's daughters was at the meeting, and I had the experience of meeting her again when I represented New Zealand at the International Conference for Women's Aglow in Anaheim,

## Royal Encounter

California, in 1985, and we were both carrying the flags of our nations. I met her in the foyer of the large arena where the conference was held, and as I went to curtsy, she said, 'Not here, not here. I'm just Siku while I am here!'

We attended the local parish church while in Tonga, and the singing was glorious because they sang in ten-part harmony with no musical background. The other thing we noticed was that most people were wearing white, which was particularly a custom for attending church on Sundays.

One day while we were in Tonga, we took a bus to go to a beach area to let our boys have a swim and a picnic. We were instructed to return to the bus departure area by 3:00 p.m. because that was when the last bus for the day left. We though we got back there on time, but unfortunately, the bus had already left, so we began walking. We were probably ten miles away from where we were staying, and the boys were not very happy about having to walk. But we trekked through a village where the children had just come out of school for the day and were following us along, calling out 'Palagi, Palagi and Palagi family' and counting our boys out loud! Apparently, it was uncommon to see white people with that number of children. Palagi (pronounced Palangi) refers to a white person.

We were trudging on the road through some banana plantations when a twin-cab Ute pulled up. The driver was a man whom Peter had been introduced to some nights earlier at a football club meeting. He said, 'Peter, I thought it was you. As I've driven through the villages, I heard the people saying the Palagi family are out walking for the good of their health!' He kindly drove us back to where we were staying with Alex's family.

## Life in High Definition

Following our two-week stay with the Tui'tavak'i family, we said our emotional goodbyes, then boarded a plane and flew to Western Samoa to spend time with the family of the children we had hosted.

The father of the family was a Magistrate who would regularly do a Court circuit around the islands of Western Samoa. We were included on this trip, which was wonderful because we got to explore more of their country. One place we visited was a lava field from a volcanic eruption, which was quite an amazing experience. Particularly, the site where the lava had flowed up to and around a church building but didn't burn the building or demolish it. The same thing happened around one grave, known as the grave of the virgin, where a young girl had been buried. We were shown where to go to the swimming pools, but not realising that they were segregated, I was in the men's pool with the boys when one of the locals came and told me I had to get out and not be there. The women's pool was further down the track!

We also climbed the mountain to visit the tomb of author Robert Louis Stevenson, located at the top of the hill. We made this climb late in the afternoon, which was a big mistake because it was so warm that we were nearly exhausted by the time we reached the top. However, it was worth the effort because of the magnificent views of the city of Apia and the surrounding country we saw from that perspective.

Returning to New Zealand, we very quickly settled into life in the Timaru Community Church. There were Bible studies, church services, and other activities, such as working and serving in the community, that kept us busy. We made many new friends and saw many people come to trust Jesus Christ as their Lord and Saviour.

One of the visiting speakers at the church was a woman who spoke prophetic words. She had one for Peter, stating that he would have a wealth of treasure and words to share with people, speaking with words of wisdom and encouraging many. We didn't realise at the time that it would become our experience in the future.

Life is not static; change happens. We were approached by Pastors from the Elim denomination in New Zealand about joining their network. This brought about some changes in leadership, as our friends who had been pastoring the church since its inception believed God was leading them to move to Australia. Our other friends who were part of the leadership team, took on the responsibility for a few months, but then believed they were to return to Christchurch. This necessitated somebody being brought in to pastor the church as Peter had not completed his diploma to become a Pastor and was still working in Telecom at the time, while I had completed my Diploma of Theology. We were interim pastors in the church for three months before a new family arrived. Life was full.

Once the new pastor and his family were settled into the church and life in a new town, we believed it was time for a change for us, and Peter was applying for positions with Telecom in other parts of the country. Eventually, a position became available in Blenheim at the top of the South Island, and we moved there in December 1985. This coincided with my representing New Zealand for Women's AGLOW at the International Convention in Anaheim, California.

We moved to Blenheim and settled into the local Elim church there, with four of the boys going with us as Michael was living in Christchurch and Chris elected to stay in Timaru. Three of the boys were enrolled in high school. Shane wanted to develop his skills on the keyboard as he wanted to use computers, but at the boys' high school, there were no typing classes, so twice a week he would bike across to the girls' high school to take typing classes, the only boy in the class. He was always willing to try new things. And Daniel started attending the local Christian School attached to the church, where we quickly began to make new friends.

During our time in Blenheim, we felt that we were only there for a season, and this was confirmed by a scripture that the Lord gave me in **Acts 28:30-31**.

During those two years, Peter and I were members of the worship team. I was on the pastoral care team. We hosted a Bible study and prayer meeting in our home, and I would meet with some of the ladies from church for exercise, Coffee and catch up during the week.

> **Acts 28:30-31** *For the next two years, Paul lived in Rome at his own expense. He welcomed all who visited him, boldly proclaiming the Kingdom of God and teaching about the Lord Jesus Christ. And no one tried to stop him.*

In 1987, our second son, Chris, was working at a mussel farm in the Marlborough Sounds and he would ride his motorbike in to visit us over the weekend. On one trip he was involved in an accident, colliding with a car on the winding road and suffered a badly broken leg—femur, fibula and tibia! He had to be airlifted to the hospital as it was too far for an ambulance to drive. When I got to the hospital (Peter was away on a men's camp that weekend) it was distressing to see the state Chris was in, but he was more concerned that the staff had cut his jeans off to work on his leg! He spent several weeks recovering with us before deciding he would rather work in town than out in the Marlborough Sounds. He had also met a young lady named Ilka, which was a further incentive to relocate!

We knew our time in Blenheim was coming to an end in December 1987 with a Word from God.

Chapter 7

# New Frontier.
## Deuteronomy 8:7

# Life in High Definition

Learning to hear God's voice was about responding to the prompting of that inner voice or knowing. Also, the prompting to read a particular scripture when needing a response or an answer for a circumstance. One such incident occurred on a Sunday morning in the church in Blenheim in December 1987. Peter handed me his Bible and tapped a verse of scripture, **Deuteronomy chapter 8:7**. My immediate thought was, '*This is Australia. And does this mean we have to go to Mount Isa?*' Which I knew was a mining area.

> **Deuteronomy 8:7**
> *For the Lord your God is bringing you into a good land. A land of brooks of water fountains and springs that flow out of the valley and hills. A land of wheat and barley, of vines and fig trees and pomegranates. A land of olive oil and honey. A land which you will eat bread without scarcity, and which you will lack nothing. A land whose stones are iron, and out of whose hills you can dig copper.*

Fortunately, we were able to make the choice of where we would live and friends that we had started the Church with, in Timaru, had moved to Melbourne in Victoria, so we relocated there in March 1988. Leaving behind Michael, who was living in Christchurch, and Chris, who was now living in town following his accident. Shane had already preceded us, moving to Sydney to work, being apprenticed to my brother Robin who had his own roof plumbing business. We arrived in Melbourne with three boys: Gerrard, Damian, and Daniel.

Our friends in Victoria had arranged for some temporary accommodation until we could find something more suitable, which fortunately only took two weeks. Some of their other friends were

## New Frontier. Deuteronomy 8:7

moving to America for work and had arranged to rent out their home during their absence for eighteen months. Unfortunately, the people they were going to rent to were not able to take up the offer, so we were introduced to them, and shortly after were able to move into their property. We still had to wait for the container with the small amount of goods we had been able to bring from New Zealand to arrive by ship. We spent about three weeks sleeping on mattresses on the floor before our container arrived.

In the meantime, we had settled the boys into the local high school. And Gerrard discovered that he had already completed the exams they were currently studying for, while we were in New Zealand. So, he said, 'I'm not staying at school, I'm going to leave.'

We told him he couldn't leave without having a job, so he found a position as an apprentice at a craftsman cabinet maker and began his new role on the other side of the city. This required him to have three bus changes to get to and return from work.

Peter found a position as a part-time document contractor, and I started work as a part-time doctor's receptionist. We were quickly able to gather enough money to buy Gerrard a car, which made it easier and quicker for him to commute to and from work. In his first year of apprenticeship, he built us a beautiful mahogany 4-poster bed, which looked very grand in our bedroom.

When we left New Zealand, Peter had taken six months leave without pay from Telecom and when that time was nearly up, he wrote and applied for redundancy, which was refused. He decided that he would return and apply in person. So, in August 1988, he flew back to New Zealand. When he arrived at work on the day he was due back, he found the Senior Supervisor was writing out a resignation letter for him, but no offer of redundancy! As Peter had worked for Telecom for twenty-four years, he believed that he was entitled to it, so he stayed on until they were willing to make the payment.

In September 1988, we received the awful news that my young sister Carmel, her husband and two young children had been involved in a serious accident. Tragically, her little daughter, Cherish, just two years old, had been killed in the accident. They had been taken to hospital in Dunedin, and I decided I needed to be there to support my sister in her time of loss and grief, so I arranged to fly to New Zealand. The boys assured me that they would be okay while I was away. Peter met me up at the airport in Christchurch, and we drove to Dunedin to be with my sister. When I saw her, she was almost unrecognisable.

Her face was so swollen and cut all over by glass from the shattered windscreen. A shaft of glass had gone into one of her eyes. And she was seven months pregnant with her third child. They had managed to stop the labour that was threatening, as she was only in her $7^{th}$ month. I'm so glad I was there to be able to help bathe her and care for her. My brother-in-law, her husband, had injured his arm, and some flesh had been removed when the car rolled over.

My sister told me something amazing. She said that she had felt people lifting her out of the car. My brother-in-law insisted that nobody had helped them, but my sister said she knew that there had been hands lifting her out of the car through the broken windscreen. I believe there were angels present, helping to preserve her life. Because after the accident, the car caught on fire. Their little boy Bodine had fallen between the seats in the car and was able to be removed safely from the car with not a scratch on him.

After two weeks in New Zealand, it was time for me to return to Australia. It was very hard leaving my sister and then Peter. Not knowing when I would see either of them again. But as the plane flew in over the coast of Australia. I saw the lights of the city, and tears welled up in my eyes, and I just had the strongest sense. God, I'm coming home. The Lord had already established in me that this was to be our home.

Peter continued his work until March 1989. When the senior supervisor came to him one day and said, 'When do you want to leave?'

And Peter asked, 'Am I getting redundancy?'

The supervisor replied, 'Yes, when do you want to leave?'

Peter said, 'Yesterday!' However, the fact that he was still in New Zealand was a blessing. When Chris had to go back into hospital for further surgery on his leg from the previous motorbike accident. Where healing had not taken place and he had to have a bone graft. And Peter was able to be there to support him during that time.

When he returned to Australia in April 1989, friends provided a holiday rental for us in Mildura on the border between Victoria and New South Wales. We had a lovely week of relaxation and time together.

We settled into life in our new host country and joined our friends at the little local church, which met in a restaurant complex near our home, while also enjoying the fellowship and getting to know other local Christians. Within a year, our friends were prompted by the Lord to return to New Zealand.

Peter accepted the responsibility for leading the local church as Pastor, and, of course, I was included in the responsibility. We joined the network of churches called the Full Gospel Churches of Australia and so began our life of Ministry in Australia.

## Life in High Definition

We've reached more milestones along the way, celebrating our 25th wedding anniversary in 1991 with a lovely surprise dinner with family and friends. And in 1994 we became Australian citizens.

After a year of serving as a pastor and working, Peter was finding it a little difficult being an autonomous Church. Another local pastor offered to join with us. This started a relationship that had some consequences for our family, as their daughter Kaylene and our son Gerrard fell in love, and were eventually married in 1993. Both were actively involved in the church, Gerrard as the drummer and Kaylene as worship leader.

A year earlier, we had celebrated the wedding of Shane to his lovely Petra. The wedding took place in Wollongong, NSW, with Peter officiating. Our family was expanding, and we were delighted to visit with them in their apartment in Sydney.

Life was full. Peter was working part-time in an electronics company as well as a pastor at the church, and I was working part-time as a doctor's receptionist as well as studying and being involved in the local Women's Ministry. Shane and Petra came to spend Christmas and up to New Year with us in 1994, and we had a lovely time together as a family with lots of laughter, storytelling, and jokes before they drove back to Sydney.

In January, Peter and I flew to New Zealand for a lovely and relaxing one-month holiday, visiting family and spending quality time together. God has ways of providing for us in preparation for things to come, as upon our return to Melbourne, we settled back into our work routines and church life. Then, on the 12th of February, we received a call that no parent ever wants to receive, from Petra to say that Shane was killed in a freak accident.

## New Frontier. Deuteronomy 8:7

He had gone out fishing with a friend from church on Sunday afternoon, to a place where the only access to the fishing spot was by climbing ropes that had been bolted onto the Cliff face, south of the Entrance to Sydney Harbour. They had enjoyed several hours of fishing but climbing back up the ropes again, Shane found it exhausting and said he didn't think he could carry on as he rested on a ledge about halfway up the 100-metre cliff. The friend took all the gear up and came back to assist Shane, but unfortunately, he held on to the wrist that had his watch on, and it slipped. Shane fell to his death.

We had to get to Sydney ASAP to be there to support Petra and to process this appalling news. Petra's sister lived in Melbourne and so she arranged to travel with me, and we flew to Sydney together with Peter driving up with the rest of the family in the car. The whole experience was so surreal. I had cried out to the Lord for some understanding about this dreadful situation. I was led to read **Psalm 94...**

> **Psalm 94:18** *I cried out my foot was slipping, but your unfailing love, oh Lord, supported me. When doubts filled my mind, your comfort gave me consolation of great joy.*

Even during such sorrow, there were some lighter moments, one of them being when we were speaking to the Undertaker, and they asked what wording we wanted to use for the newspaper notification of death. One of the boys suggested, Fell off a Cliff!

Chapter 8

# OPEN DOOR!
# Just in Time.
# Jeremiah 1:5

## Life in High Definition

Returning to Melbourne, we all tried to settle into routine again, but it was difficult. I seemed to walk around in a fog much of the time, and my heart hurt all the time. A friend came to visit, carrying a bucket with cleaning materials, and said, 'I've come to do your floors and your bathrooms.' I protested that it wasn't necessary, but she said, 'This is what I believe I'm to do for you.' It was a great help because there were so many days when I just walked around in circles.

Peter was functioning at his part-time job in electronics as a workplace chaplain. He found himself speaking with some of the men there who had gone through the experience of loss and grief with the death of family members.

We decided both of us needed to have a time out and elected to go and spend what would have been Shane's birthday in May with Petra in Sydney. We then took some time out for us to rest and recover, deciding to just drive without any specific destination in mind. In June 1995, while we were driving north into Queensland, we received notification of a conference that was taking place in Sydney. And we really believe that we needed to be there.

After travelling for a month visiting Far North Queensland, we returned to Sydney to attend the conference. This was a life-changing experience for me again; taking an opportunity to be prayed for, I found myself experiencing the joy of being set free from a spirit of grief. And I had the sense that I had been hearing from the Lord that this had been in my life since my very conception. To transition from walking around with a feeling of a broken heart to being full of joy was a wonderful experience.

Following our return to Victoria, I had a real sense that the Lord was prompting me to read the book of Jeremiah 1:5. It was a 'rhema' word for me, I had the strongest sense then that God was telling me

# OPEN DOOR! Just in Time. Jeremiah 1:5

I needed to go through the process of becoming an ordained pastor, working alongside my husband Peter in the local church. This was confirmed for me by a mentor and senior pastor of the movement that we were involved with at the time, The Full Gospel Churches of Australia, when we attended a Conference and Peter and I shared my thoughts with him.

> **Jeremiah 1:5** *I knew you before you were formed in your mother's womb. Before you were born, I set you apart and appointed you as a prophet to the nations.*

He immediately had me fill out the necessary paperwork. The ceremony took place in August 1995, and it was a wonderful day, my family and the Church family gathered, a celebration of responding to God's leading.

The next few months were very enlightening and encouraging as I discovered more of the truth of the Bible and my responsibilities as a pastor. The friends we were sharing the leadership of the church with decided it was time for them to move into another area and start a congregation there. And so, it was back to just Peter and I serving in the local church.

The electronics company Peter was working part-time for decided to relocate to NSW. And so, a period of him being away during the week and returning every weekend became our life for the next couple of months, which meant I had most of the day-to-day responsibility for the church. I was grateful to have the support of some wonderful people on our team.

The commuting began to take a toll on Peter's health, so he decided that it was time to relinquish that job and take on pastoring the church full-time. This was a significant step of faith for us, given that we didn't have a regular income, but we saw the provision of God daily.

We had become friends with some local pastors, Graham and Susan McMechan who were members of the Ministers Fellowship International Network. And they invited us to a conference and then asked if we would like to join them. Peter and I believed that was our next step of faith and so became another period of more study and learning, and some wonderful mentoring and teaching. We undertook a seminar study called the Key of Knowledge, which gave us more skills on preaching and teaching the Bible. I also enrolled in a local Bible college for a course being offered there. Following this, I had a prompting from the Lord that I was to undertake a degree course that they were offering. Eventually, I received my Bachelor of Ministry degree in 2005.

Prior to this, in 1998, we celebrated the wedding of our youngest son, Daniel and Catherine in January (on a 42°c day!). The next day, I flew to Florida, USA, for a conference at Brownsville, where there had been a revival happening for several months, joining my friend Susan and others who had preceded me. Following the conference, Susan and I flew to England for three days as this was included in our travel arrangements. I still remember how wonderful it was to visit Buckingham Palace, Westminster Cathedral, Piccadilly Square, and Harrods!

As we were staying with friends outside of London, we had an adventure one day when we boarded the wrong train and ended up on our way to Portsmouth! Fortunately for us (but not for all the other commuters!), the train experienced some problems and had to stop at a remote country station. There just happened to be a train going in the direction we needed, so after a mad dash down the platform we ended up getting to our destination!

## OPEN DOOR! Just in Time. Jeremiah 1:5

Flying back to Melbourne was wonderful as it was great to be back with Peter and the family. I settled into studying and reconnecting with the people, and we received the news that we were going to be grandparents again with Daniel and Catherine's first child expected by the end of the year. We also met the new partner of our younger son, Damian, Deborah and her son Aden. And we welcomed them into the family with their wedding in July 2000.

In March and April 2000, we were blessed with two more grandies, Orianna, born to Damian and Deb, and Jackson, born to Daniel and Catherine.

As I was a credentialed minister able to conduct marriages, I was asked if I would be prepared to officiate a wedding in a Hot Air Balloon! I thought that would be a highlight, and I was not wrong! We floated above the Yarra Valley, enveloped in the dissolving mist, with just eight of us in the basket: the pilot, myself as Minister, the bride and groom, their two witnesses, and a parent of each of the couple. The pilot and I worked out a system where he would nod to me when he needed to fire a burst of fuel into the burner so I could pause speaking!

Before that happy event, however, we had experienced another tragedy. The cot death of Daniel and Catherine's second little boy, Jackson, just three months after he was born. This was so heartbreaking to receive the news. And when I cried out to the Lord, asking how this could happen to such a bonny, healthy baby, He led me to Psalm 23:4.

> **Psalm 23:4** *Even though I walk through the darkest valley, I will not be afraid, for you are close beside me. Your rod and your staff protect and comfort me.*

# Life in High Definition

It was a hard time, but life went on, and we received the news that they were expecting another baby in 2001, and we were soon welcoming baby Dylan, who was born in June that year.

In 2002, on Australia Day, I had just conducted a wedding locally for a couple in our congregation. When we returned home, we received a phone call from Chris's partner, Ilka, in New Zealand. He had been involved in a motorbike accident and was seriously injured. They were flying him to Wellington from Nelson but didn't expect him to live as he had a serious head injury and many broken bones.

Peter immediately arranged for a flight to Wellington, New Zealand. I desperately wanted to travel with him, but Damian needed to go more than I did because he was still experiencing grief after the death of his brother Shane. The next ten days were a succession of miracles. When Peter arrived in the middle of the night, he asked the staff what the most serious issue was, and they explained there was bleeding in his brain, and he would have to go into the theatre first thing in the morning to have his skull opened. Peter anointed him, prayed for him, went away to sleep for the night, then came back at 9:00 a.m. the next day to find Chris still connected to all the tubes and cords. He asked what was happening, and they said it was interesting. During the middle of the night, the bleeding stopped. The first miracle.

From that point on, every day Chris was anointed and prayed for. Other healing took place as well; a spine fractured in three places, for which there was no longer any evidence, and a punctured lung, causing problems with breathing, was restored. After spiking a temperature for several days, they discovered that he had bitten through his tongue in the accident and needed to get him into the theatre to fix it, but there was no room in any theatre. Peter prayed, and fifteen minutes later they took Chris away to the theatre. They told us he would have to learn to talk again, but when he came out of the coma, he was able to speak as well as before. It was another miracle.

Two weeks later, Chris was flown back to the hospital in Nelson. When the nurse on duty arrived, she looked at his chart and said, 'Chris Allen, no, it's not the same person.'

He said, 'Yes, that's me.'

And she said, 'Oh no, the Chris Allen that was in here was in a motorbike accident and he was flown to Wellington.'

He said, 'Yes, that's me.'

And she said, 'Oh, I don't believe it, we thought you died!'

Following his release from the hospital, Chris spent some months in recovery. He had to redo all the licences that he held, and preparing to return to work, which he was able to do in less than a year. It was all quite miraculous after such a horrendous accident. Unfortunately, his relationship with Ilka, the mother of their children, did not survive this crisis. And in late 2002 they parted company.

Eventually, Chris and Kim got together. She had also gone through a broken relationship, but the children all went to school together. They began to keep company and eventually decided to marry. And I had the privilege of officiating their wedding in 2009. Such a special day with their four children as their attendants.

Chapter 9

# HOMELESS! Survival.
## Jeremiah 29:11-14

# Life in High Definition

Following our trip to New Zealand, after Peter's release from the hospital in 2008, the situation changed for us, as we had been house sharing with our youngest son and his wife. They needed to be closer to a school where both boys could walk there each day, and we needed to find somewhere else to live, but at the time, there was nothing available. We essentially became homeless.

In the middle of all this happening, we also had to close the church. Because of Peter's surgery and Gerrard's death, our hope that Daniel would become a pastor was not realised, so we had to process that grief as well. We were blessed to see our church family find other congregations that welcomed them in.

Then, friends who lived in central Queensland were going overseas on a six-month mission trip and asked us to house-sit for them. Thank you for the provision, Lord.

We set out on our journey to Emerald in central Queensland. Peter dropped me off at the airport in Sydney on the way, where I met with my friend and fellow pastor, Olga, as we were flying to South Africa to speak at a Women's conference. We were there for two weeks experiencing African culture and spending time with local Christian leaders, visiting some of the townships where they were providing a feeding programme and teaching ministry.

In the meantime, Peter had driven to Emerald by himself, and he and David had managed to look after themselves until Olga and I returned. We spent quality time with David and Olga Kirk. Olga was the Pastor of the local Church, and we had become friends as soon as we met them several years earlier at a Minister's Fellowship conference in Melbourne.

# HOMELESS! Survival. Jeremiah 29:11-14

The surgeon's comments about it being too soon to go travelling were followed up in months to come when Peter was supposed to be having monthly appointments at the clinic. When the surgeon said, 'Now we'll see you in a month's time, are you going to be in the country?' We would not be. Peter was determined that he was not going to allow this condition to hold him back.

Following our time in central Queensland, we returned to Victoria and spent a few weeks with our daughter-in-law, Kaylene and her son Connor. Then it became necessary for us to find a place for ourselves. Unfortunately, rental accommodation was scarce at the time.

I prayed. Asking the Lord for some direction, I was led to the scripture in **Jeremiah 29:11**, where the Lord said He had the plans for our future, and he prompted me to contact a prayer ministry.

> **Jeremiah 29:11** *For I know the plans I have for you, says The Lord. They are plans for good and not disaster, to give you a future and a hope.*

When I spoke to the woman involved, she said, 'Oh, we need someone to manage a crisis accommodation, are you interested? I think you would be ideal for the job.' This began a new chapter in our lives. Living on site, helping women and their children escaping domestic violence or other circumstances requiring them to be in a safe place. It was a whole new learning curve for us. But an opportunity to encourage, support and share faith with these people who were struggling.

During that time, we also experienced some heartbreak ourselves with Daniel and Catherine's marriage not surviving the death of their little boy, Jackson, even with the arrival of their younger son, Dylan.

# Life in High Definition

They had relocated to Queensland, but the strain had been too much for them. So, Daniel returned to Victoria for work, and after some months, they attempted a reconciliation, but it didn't work and so, they ended up divorcing. This was a true heartbreak to us.

During this time, Damian and Deborah, along with their family, had relocated to Darwin in the Northern Territory for his work. This was a big adventure for them and a scary time as Damian ended up having a blood clot after playing squash, causing a pulmonary embolism while he was on location in Alice Springs for work.

Fortunately, he had gone to a doctor to check out the pain in his leg, and he was immediately sent to the local hospital. And the embolism happened while he was there, so they were able to resuscitate him, praise God! They also gave us another two 'grandies' while they were there, Elsie Mae, born on her late uncle Shane's birthday, the 11th of May 2003, and Imogen Grace born on the 19th of April 2005, just two days after my mother, her great grandmother's birthday!

We lived on site at the crisis accommodation for twelve months. And then a unit became available for Peter and me, which we deemed was the right time for us to move. So, we found a young woman named Kristy who came and managed the property, and we quickly became friends. We remained on the board and organising committee for the property for a period of five years before the Lord opened the door for us to move to Queensland.

We had been invited to house-sit for friends in Hervey Bay, north of Brisbane, who were going overseas for six weeks. Peter had not been 100% before we left Victoria due to the cold weather, and within three days had ended up in the hospital. Our friends set off on their trip while Peter was in the hospital for a few days before being released.

## HOMELESS! Survival. Jeremiah 29:11-14

When they returned six weeks later, he was a picture of health. And their comment was: 'You need to move to Queensland; he obviously needs the warmer weather up here.'

As we had no financial resources, we approached the Government housing department for help in getting accommodation. And then had to return to Victoria, believing that it would be two or three months before we would move. We returned to Victoria, and Peter ended up in hospital again!

This was due to him overdosing on one of the medications he had been given and not taking another because of confusion with containers. While he was in the hospital, I received a call from the housing department in Queensland to say that your supporting documentation cannot be from Victoria; you need to have something with a local address. If you can get here in twenty-eight days, we will be able to help you.

We were there in twenty-seven days after a whirlwind of packing, selling furniture and downsizing. Damian was going to drive us, towing a trailer provided by one of our other sons, Daniel, who worked for a trailer hire company. Unfortunately, at the last minute, Damian was unable to drive us, as he had made a previous commitment to a Scout activity, so we scrambled to find something suitable as an alternative. Everything was so expensive, but we managed to locate a two-tonne vehicle on a one-way hire. We crammed both the van and the car to the hilt, with Peter driving the van and myself driving the car, we set off on our journey. It took us three days to drive to Hervey Bay, and we were exhausted by the time we got there, but we made it! Our friends helped us put everything into storage until we could find a suitable place to live.

We were thankful to the Lord for His promise in **Jeremiah 29**, giving us a future and a hope. The Housing Department could not provide

## Life in High Definition

us with anywhere to live, so we found some private accommodation and moved into a lovely locality beside a lagoon. We enjoyed watching all the Bird Life and native animals that would come to the water, and they were right on our doorstep. There truly was so much to enjoy.

We found a lively Church Community and settled in with them. Life was good, and within a year, a new pastor was to be appointed to the church, Pastor David Davies, with his wife, Tracey, and their seven children. When we met him and he found out that we were retired pastors, he said, 'I've got a role for you. I'm going to form a pastoral care team, and I would really like you to be part of it.' And thus began a new role of, again, caring for and supporting people and working as a team.

We also took on the responsibility of looking after the seniors in the church community, and we called the group The Good Life. We would meet on a regular basis for teaching and encouragement, and for coffee dates. Of course, living in Hervey Bay meant being able to go down to the beach and find a spot where we could enjoy the fresh air and sunshine was a bonus.

It was a wonderful life, and we made lots of new friends. People were entertained by Peter's wonderful sense of humour, asking what the newest story was each week when we met for prayer, study, or coffee.

Just months after shifting to Queensland, we drove back to Victoria to celebrate the wedding of our dear daughter-in-law, Kaylene, to her new husband, Rob. What a wonderful day and such a joy to see her happy after being on her own raising Connor for the previous eight years. While there, we caught up with other family and friends.

Chapter 10

# Time out.
## Psalm 71:20-21

## Life in High Definition

2016 saw us celebrating our fiftieth wedding anniversary and we were blessed to be given a trip to England to spend time with our eldest son Michael (known as Mike in England!) and his lovely Julia. We had six wonderful weeks with them, visiting some beautiful places in Devon and Cornwall, Surrey, Somerset, Essex, and Hertfordshire, as well as London City. We also enjoyed getting to know Julia's parents and her sister, Gillian. Our last day in England on that trip was Guy Fawkes Day, and they do bonfires and fireworks in a big way for that event, which was a great way to celebrate Mike's birthday! We were rugged up like polar bears because it was so cold, but it was magnificent seeing the display that was set off. The next day, we flew back to Australia.

Returning to Hervey Bay, we settled into life in the local church and enjoyed the warm climate and the relaxed lifestyle. However, some of the issues that Peter had because of the surgery and all the stress and grief that we had gone through, his health began to deteriorate. And so, we experienced several trips to the hospital.

Unfortunately, on one of those trips, he had already had a small dressing on his leg, but the dressing was left on the leg for several days and removed all the skin from his calf to his ankle. It took us nearly eighteen months to get that restored and healed. And it was only due to New Zealand manuka honey that, eventually, all the skin was restored on his leg. During this time, in response to more prayer for Peter, I was led to a promise in **Psalm 71**...

In 2018, a cardiologist took me aside and said, 'Peter's heart is failing and there's nothing we can do about it because he's had the laryngectomy.' I couldn't see why they couldn't do a surgery and fix his heart, but they were not prepared to take the risk. We took a train trip to Cairns in July to visit Damian, Deborah, and the family. When we returned from Cairns, Peter had another trip to the hospital, and

## Time out. Psalm 71:20-21

> **Psalm 71:20-21** *You have allowed me to suffer much hardship, but you will restore me to life again and lift me up from the depths of the earth. You will restore me to even greater honour and comfort me once again.*

this time experienced some more harm from procedures and just wanted to be at home. His strength gave out on the 20$^{th}$ of September, and he was taken to the hospital again. I believe he was just so tired of it all that in the early hours on the 21$^{st}$ he went home to heaven. When I spoke to the doctor, he tried to explain that Peter had asked to be sat up and just became non-responsive. Part of me was glad that his suffering was over, but the rest of me was struggling with how I could go on without him. After 53 years together, I felt lost.

Before Peter was taken to the hospital, we had a visit from Daniel and his new girlfriend, Flor, from the Philippines. During their visit, he had proposed to her. She had to return for a month to the Philippines but had assured me that she would come back and help me look after Pop. By the time she came back, of course, we had already had the Memorial and celebration service with the rest of the family gathered from around the country, including Mike & Julia from England.

When Flor returned from the Philippines, she and Daniel had already planned to marry, so a month after Peter died, I officiated the wedding for Daniel and Flor at our favourite beach, in Hervey Bay. I then flew to Sydney to spend two weeks with my sister, giving the newlyweds the place to themselves, and I virtually slept for a whole week!

We adjusted to our new lifestyle, Dan and Flor, living with me and both looking for work, while I kept myself busy working on the pastoral care team at the church and leading the seniors group.

Chapter 11

# Mandates and Mayhem!
## Jeremiah 15:20

## Life in High Definition

The year 2020, a time I'm sure many would rather forget, began with lockdowns and coercive government control, including masks and injections to combat the so-called 'pandemic'. As time and careful study has proven, this was a devised strategy to control nations, not heal them! When I asked the Lord for His response as I refused to wear a mask, I received Jeremiah 15:20.

> **Jeremiah 15:20** *They will fight against you like an attacking army, but I will make you as secure as a fortified wall of bronze. They will not conquer you, for I am with you to protect and rescue you. I The Lord have spoken!*

Dan and Flor, however, were struggling as mandates were enacted, forcing people to comply or face losing their jobs. Dan would not be injected, but Flor was, which in turn led to periods of sickness for her.

Over the next eighteen months Dan could not get full time work although he was giving many volunteer hours to the church with the food warehouse with driving, etc. Due to lack of income Dan and Flor decided to move further south where full-time work was available for them both. This led to me being unable to continue living in the unit I called home as the rents sky-rocketed in Hervey. By 2023, I knew I could not renew my lease and began selling off furniture and packing to move, not knowing where I was to live!

In January, I received a devastating phone call from Chris in New Zealand; his only son, Cody, had taken his own life. He had battled with drug problems for several years and it just got too much for him. My oldest grandson was gone in his thirtieth year. I flew to New Zealand to be with the family, and it was so hard seeing my son go through the pain I had experienced twice. The consolation God gave

## Mandates and Mayhem! Jeremiah 15:20

me from His Word was Joel 2:32 But everyone who calls on the name of the Lord will be saved. The one consolation for Chris and Kim, Ilka, who is Cody's mother, and Josie, who is Cody's sister, were the two dear little boys, Jesse and Riley, that Cody had fathered.

> **Joel 2:32** *But everyone who calls on the name of the Lord will be saved.*

Returning to Hervey Bay, I had plenty to keep me busy with Church responsibilities and downsizing in preparation for moving, not knowing where to!

At our regional Ministry conference that year, my friend Alan came and asked how I was getting on with accommodation, and I replied I had no idea where I was going, but I was getting ready for the door the Lord would open for me, and he said, 'God already told us to get a place ready for you!' He owned a property south of Brisbane that had previously been a Christian camp, so there were several units on the property.

I moved there in December 2023 with Dan, loading what I had left onto his Ute and trailer and moving it for me. A lighter note to the whole experience, as I had to stay in Hervey Bay for a further week, I had drawn a plan of the bedsitter for Dan to show him where to put my few pieces of furniture. When he phoned me after delivering it, he said, 'Your plan was bigger!'

One of the positive things about my new location was that it was only 30 minutes away from where Dan and Flor were now living out West, instead of the four to five hours it had previously been from Hervey Bay.

## Life in High Definition

I moved to my new location and immediately packed a suitcase and flew to New Zealand where my eldest great-grandson Jesse was having his 5th birthday. I then went on to Timaru, my old stamping ground, where the church was having its 40th year celebration. And I was able to share some of our experiences from the beginning at the celebration.

Returning to my new home in the country, I was sitting and wondering what I was going to do with myself now that I was completely on my own in this little place.

As I was praying, having just had my 77th birthday, the Lord reminded me that I had surrendered my life to Him in 1977, and that this year was going to be a year of double blessing for me.

I began to receive phone calls: Will you come and speak at our church? Will you come and help here? Our senior ministers for my ministry network rang and asked would I be prepared to go and help some friends down in Victoria who needed some support for a time? So, I ended up spending a month in Victoria over the winter. Fortunately, the home I was staying in had a good heating system as it was incredibly cold compared to QLD.

Just before I drove to Victoria, Flor's three children finally arrived with her sister, Yep. It had been a very long, drawn-out process to get the health checks and paperwork done, but they made it! Yep, and LJ, who was already in High School and a top-ranked basketball player back in the Philippines, was only staying for two months, but Flonie and Nathaniel, both primary age, were here to stay. Adjusting to living in a cold climate!

Returning in time for Dan's birthday on the 19th of July. I was only home for two weeks and then drove up to Emerald in Central Queensland to be with my friend Olga for her birthday and speak at the local Church. On my return journey, I spent a few days in Hervey Bay catching up with all my dear friends there, then made the final driving stretch home. Previously, Mike and Julia had been going to fly out to Australia, but due to a change in circumstances, they were not able to come. So, I said, 'Well, if you can't come to me, then I will have to come to you!' So, arrangements were made that I would spend Christmas and New Year's with them.

After conducting a wedding at our local church and being sent out with prayers of blessing, I flew out to England on the 10th of December. It was freezing cold but was so good to see Mike and Julia again as I had not seen them since Peter passed away.

We had a wonderful time exploring as Mike was between jobs. We rode in a Hovercraft to the Isle of Wight for a few hours, visited Stonehenge, and read up on the history of the site. We also visited Salisbury Cathedral, a magnificent building with the tallest spire in England. We had an interesting experience while we were there, speaking with one of the ministers I noticed names were written over the seats in the aisle and saw one that said 'Ilfracombe', and when I remarked on this, that there was a town in Queensland with that name, the minister said, 'Oh, you come from Queensland! My grandson is out there for a surfing contest right now!' Such a small world!

We had some wonderful meals out, including 'High Tea' at The Ritz! Experienced a live play at one of the oldest theatres and zoomed around a Royal Horticultural Garden on a scooter. It was such fun and such a lovely place to visit.

I also got to try out another scooter when we went to the Brooklands Museum where Sir Stirling Moss drove his bluebird in the land speed

## Life in High Definition

record. There is also a Concorde plane there, as Brooklands was the Base for Vickers Viking aircraft manufacture, and they had also made the front of the Concorde. I now have a certificate to say that I was on the last Concorde to fly commercially. The first atmospheric pressure chamber for testing aircraft is also on site, designed by the man who developed the bouncing bombs used by the Dam Busters.

Mike and Julia live in Hertfordshire, and my first three weeks were at their home, then we transferred to Woking in Surrey for three weeks to house-sit for Julia's sister while she was away in South Africa! And look after one pampered cat named Poppy!

We had one day of snow while we were there, which was my only experience despite the freezing temperatures, so I'm glad I had my Ugg boots!

On my return trip in late January, Mike and Julia blessed me with an upgrade to Business Class from Dubai to Brisbane; the London to Dubai flight was fully booked. What a way to travel! My own recliner bed seat, lovely pj's, access to the lounge whenever I wanted, with all drinks and food supplied. Luxury!

Back to my little bedsitter and rain, rain, rain! February was action-packed, with a local conference, visiting with friends, a trip to Hervey Bay, our National MFI conference on the Gold Coast and a chance to catch up with my brother, Mike and his wife and family. There was more rain in March, and I was surrounded by water, but still able to get out and speak at my friend's Church in Pittsworth, with Pastor Brett and Sharon Dolley.

Then we had a threatening cyclone...Alfred. In the middle of the night there was a loud crash, and I thought my car had been hit. The power was off, so in the middle of the howling wind and rain, I took a torch

## Mandates and Mayhem! Jeremiah 15:20

to check on the car, all was okay! Turning around, I saw a huge tree hanging over the front of my unit. In the morning, I discovered it had come through the roof of my little bathroom...right over the shower! Praise God, the water had somewhere to drain.

Chapter 12

# The Adventure Continues.
## Philippians 4:8

## Life in High Definition

There was some doubt whether I would be able to fly to New Zealand for my granddaughter Demi's wedding in March due to the storm, but I made it! It was a glorious day for the wedding in a lovely outdoor setting as Tom and Demi were married, with one of the lovely bridesmaids being my other granddaughter, Josie.

After an enjoyable time with the family, I returned to my little place in the country to more rain! Fortunately, I had missed out on most of the disruption with power outage and howling wind, and my friend Alan had managed to remove the big tree, but there was still a hole in the roof! The Lord was making sure I kept my attitude right with His Word in Philippians 4 ...

I was only back for two weeks when I was invited to speak at my friend's Church in Emerald, Central QLD, as Pastor Tony & Helena and family were going to New Zealand for the school holidays, so on the road again, and I had a great time with my dear friends Olga and David staying on to celebrate Easter with them. While I was there, I drove up to Moranbah to catch up with Pastor Dave & Tracey, and the family who are now Pastoring in that region. It was good to see them again.

> **Philippians 4:8** *Fix your thoughts on what is true, and honorable, and right and pure and lovely, and admirable. Think about things which are excellent and worthy of praise.*

On my journey back home, I stopped off in Hervey Bay for a few days, catching up with dear friends, including Lynne Dawson & her husband, Alan and as many other friends as I could fit in. It was a pleasure meeting the new pastors at the Church too.

# The Adventure Continues. Philippians 4:8

My sister Carmel flew up from NSW for a visit, doing business stuff with Dan, so we got to spend some time together and visited brother Mike and his wife Fluff for a day as well.

I received an invitation to go to a Writer's Seminar on the Gold Coast, and I thought this could be interesting...it was!

Moving forward until today: With the amazing support and encouragement offered by Ultimate Publishing Company, I have written this book with the sincere hope that it will encourage every reader that there is a hope and a future available through God's grace following any grief, loss or tragedy.

## SALVATION PRAYER

Lord be merciful to me, a sinner.
Forgive me of my sins.

Come into my life and make me new, I believe that Jesus died on the cross for me and rose from the dead for me. Jesus I want you to be my friend and the Lord of my life and I will serve you all the days of my life, amen.

# About the Author

Leonie Allen is an ordained pastor, wife, now widowed, a mother of six sons, grandmother (known as Nonie) to twenty-two grandchildren, and great grandmother to two young boys.

Leonie was born in Dunedin, New Zealand, and is the oldest of eleven children; seven boys and four girls. While Leonie and was not close with her siblings during childhood due to being the oldest sibling, they have developed a close relationship throughout adulthood.

After a minimal secondary education (two years), Leonie trained as a telephonist working for the New Zealand post office, before leaving that job to work for her parents in their catering business where she met Peter and married at the age of nineteen. Together they produced six boys in six years and eight months, before undergoing surgery for cervical cancer when she was thirty, where Leonie had a life-changing encounter with Jesus.

## Life in High Definition

The next decade was a time of learning, study and busyness raising six boys, culminating in pastoring a congregation in New Zealand before relocating to Australia for a similar role. Leonie obtained a diploma in theology in 1985, then was ordained as a pastor in 1995 followed by a Bachelor of Ministry in 2005.

She has taught at Christian seminars and conferences both internationally and nationally.

**Peter post surgery**

**Peter prior to surgery**

**Wedding Day, June 1966**

**Young adventurers**

**Primary school photo**

**Family with Tongan son Alex**

**Shane Died February 1995**

**Leonie Ordination Day, August 1995**

**Leonie Graduation Day, 2005**

**Gerrard Died New Years Eve, 2007**

**Mother and remaining sons after Peter's funeral, 2019**

# Notes

# Life in High Definition

# Notes

# Life in High Definition

## Notes

www.ingramcontent.com/pod-product-compliance
Lightning Source LLC
Chambersburg PA
CBHW060340080526
**44584CB00013B/852**